CHANTS AND PRAYERS

Compiled and Illustrated
by Stan Padilla

The Book Publishing Company
Summertown, Tennessee

Book Publishing Company
P.O. Box 99, Summertown, TN 38483 USA
1-800-695-2241

ISBN 1-57067-020-X

Padilla, Stan, 1945-
        Chants and prayers / compiled and illustrated by Stan Padilla.
                p.   cm.
        ISBN 1-57067-020-X
        1. Indians of North America--Religion.   2. Indians of North
America--Prayer-books and devotions.   3. Indian proverbs--North
America.   I. Title.
E98.R3P225   1995
299' .74--dc20   95-42604
                                                      CIP

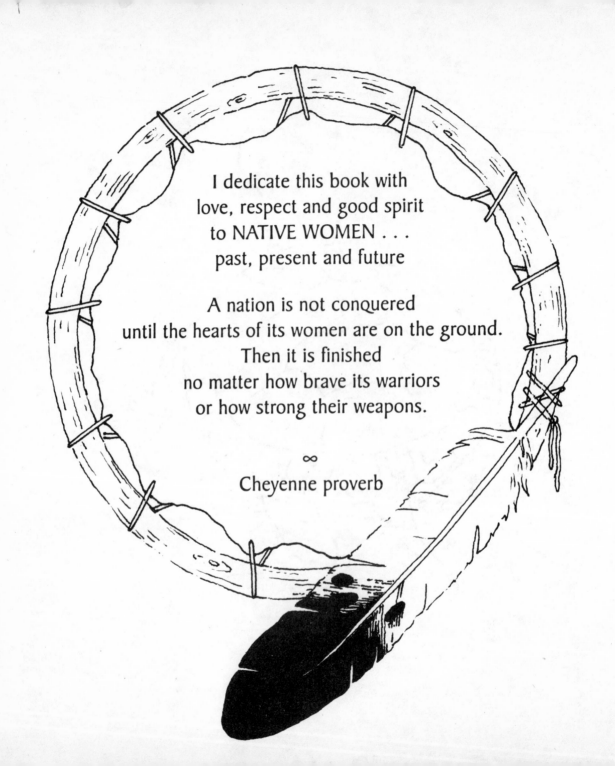

I dedicate this book with
love, respect and good spirit
to NATIVE WOMEN . . .
past, present and future

A nation is not conquered
until the hearts of its women are on the ground.
Then it is finished
no matter how brave its warriors
or how strong their weapons.

∞

Cheyenne proverb

Oh Great Spirit . . .
Whose voice I hear in the winds,
Whose breath gives life to the world, hear me . . .

I am small and weak. I need your strength and wisdom.
May I walk in beauty.

Make my eyes behold the red and purple sunset.

Make my hands respect the things you have made
and my ears sharp to hear your voice.

Make me wise so that I may know
the things you have taught your children,
the lessons you have written in every leaf and rock.

Make me strong, not to be superior to my brothers,
but to fight my greatest enemy—myself.

Make me ready to come to you with straight eyes
so that when life fades as the fading sunset
my spirit may come to you without shame.

∞

Chief Yellow Lark, Lakota 1887

Contents

Introduction

The prayers, chants, and thoughts shared in this book are rooted in Native American oral traditions and have been spoken, sung, and danced for generations. They are imbued with thousands of years of continuous culture, customs, and traditions.

In the Native American lifeways, all that is essential to life is carried within you...it is ever present in the heart. We believe the expression of what is in our hearts gives order and a center to our lives.

Prayers, chants, and spiritual thoughts help us to bring about the fulfillment of our lives. They help us to develop constructive relationships with our families, tribe, nation, and the powers of the universe. These ancient words echo the past and resound toward the future.

To many of the earliest tribes, the world was sung into being. Now as we approach the 21st century, these offerings can help us renew our relationship to the earth and "sing" a new world into being.

Keep the faith in these sacred words!

∞ *Stan Padilla,*
1995

The Tribe

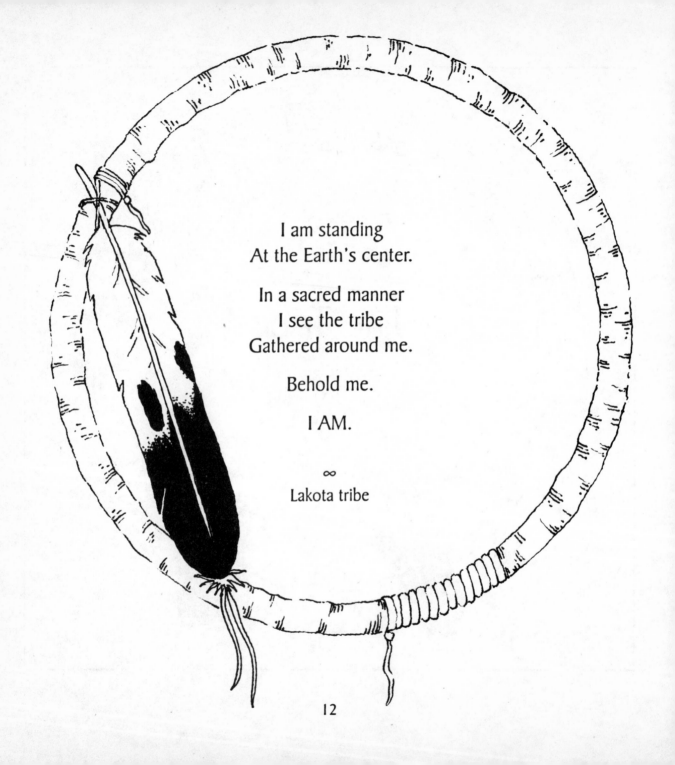

I am standing
At the Earth's center.

In a sacred manner
I see the tribe
Gathered around me.

Behold me.

I AM.

∞

Lakota tribe

12

The whole world is coming,
A nation is coming, a nation is coming,
The eagle has brought the message to the tribe.
The father says so, the father says so.
Over the whole earth they are coming.
The buffalo are coming, the buffalo are coming,
The crow has brought the message to the tribe,
The father says so, the father says so.

∞ *Lakota Ghost Dance song*

Look as they rise, rise up.
Over the line where the sky meets the earth;
Pleiades!
Lo! They are ascending, come to guide us,
Leading us safely, keeping us one;
Pleiades!
Teach us to be, like you, united.

∞ *Pawnee tribe*

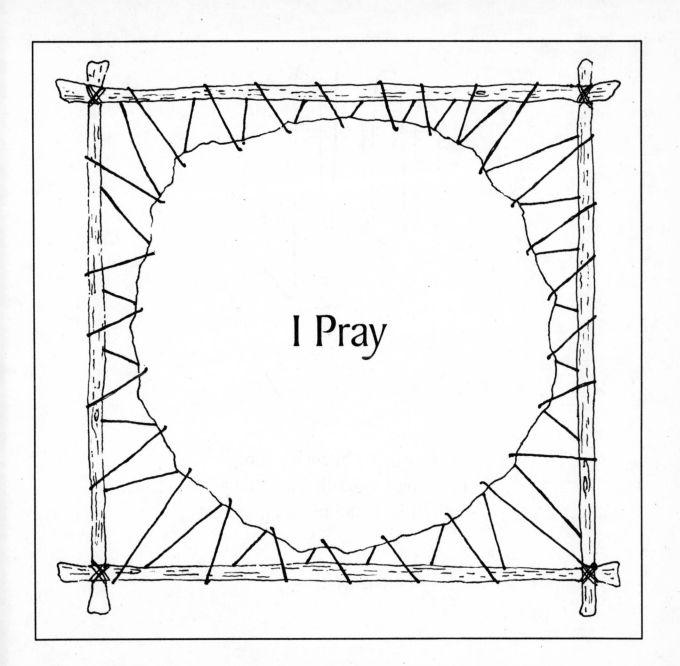

I Pray

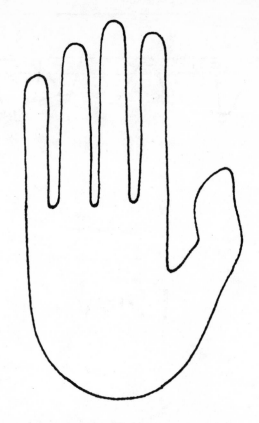

How shall I begin my song
in the blue night that is settling?
I will sit here and begin my song.

∞

Papago tribe

Grandfather:
    A Voice I am going to send!
Hear me,
All over the Universe:
    A voice I am going to send!
Hear me,
Grandfather:
    I will live!
Now I have said it.

∞ *Lakota tribe*

Friend of the Eagle,
To you I pass the pipe first.
Around the circle I pass it to you.
Around the circle I begin the day.
Around the circle I complete the fourth direction.
I pass the pipe to Grandfather above.
I smoke with the Great mystery.
So begins a good day.

∞ *Lakota pipe song*

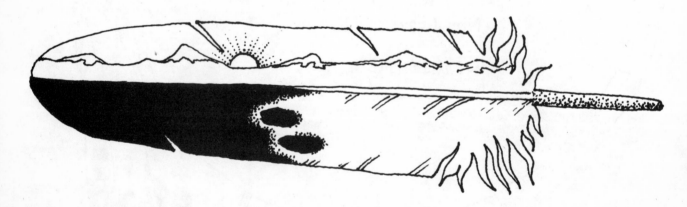

It is I who made the pipe,
Says the father, says the father.

∞

Lakota Ghost Dance song

Giving Thanks

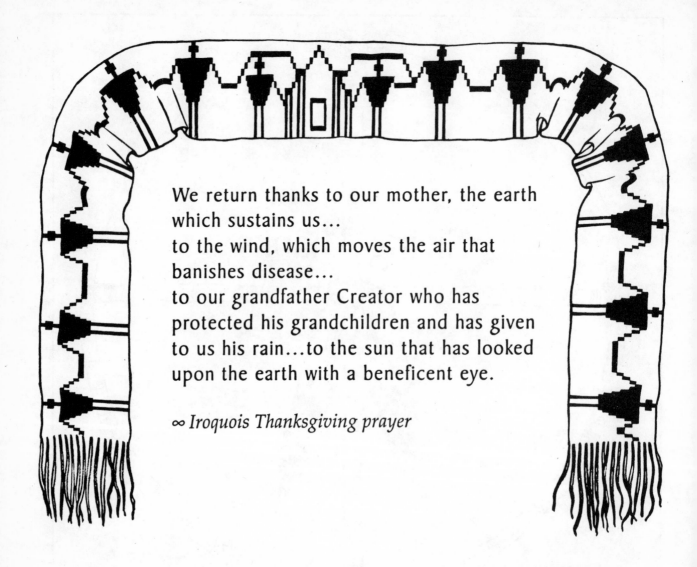

We return thanks to our mother, the earth
which sustains us...
to the wind, which moves the air that
banishes disease...
to our grandfather Creator who has
protected his grandchildren and has given
to us his rain...to the sun that has looked
upon the earth with a beneficent eye.

∞ *Iroquois Thanksgiving prayer*

My relatives, I am thankful now this day that we are thinking how the blessings come when our father, Great Spirit, remembers us, and we can see that we have lived to see together the spring time.

This is why we are thankful; when we see everything coming up and our grandfather trees, they send out buds. Now all over the universe it looks fine… Also we feel it when our elder brother, the sun, puts forth heat. He sympathizes with us and besides these our grandfather, the thunders, gave us plenty of water. All is created by our father, the Creator. Even it is said, every manitu (spirit) prays because sometimes we hear our grandfather trees, that they pray earnestly when the wind goes by.

That is enough for making anyone think and to bring happiness when one sees the wonderful works of our father, how well it affects us all year long.

∞ *Lenápe Spring prayer*

PRAYER TO MOTHER EARTH

Our Mother the Earth is lying here.
She has given of her fruitfulness.
She has given us her power.
Give thanks to Mother Earth who is lying here.

Look at Mother Earth growing fields!
Look towards the promise of her fruitfulness!
Her power she has given us.
Give thanks to Mother Earth who is lying here.

Look at Mother Earth spreading trees!
Look towards the promise of her fruitfulness!
Her power she has given us.
Give thanks to Mother Earth who is lying here.

∞

Pawnee tribe

PRAYER OF ONE MAN

I don't know if the voice of man can reach to the sky,
I don't know if the Mighty One will hear as I pray.
I don't know if the gifts I ask for will be granted.
I don't know if the word of old we truly can hear.
I don't know what will come to pass in future days.
I hope that only good will come to you.

I now know that the voice of man can reach to the sky.
I now know that the Mighty one has heard my prayer.
I now know that the gifts I have asked for have all been granted.
I now know that the word of old we can truly hear.
I now know that Spirit speaks through our prayers.
I know that only good has come to you.

∞ *Pawnee tribe*

ZUNI PRAYER

We are grateful,
  O Mother Earth
For the mountains
  and the streams
Where the deer, by command of your
Breath of life, shall wander.
Wishing for you the
fullness of life.
We shall go forth prayerfully upon
the trails of our Earth Mother.

∞ *Zuni Tribe*

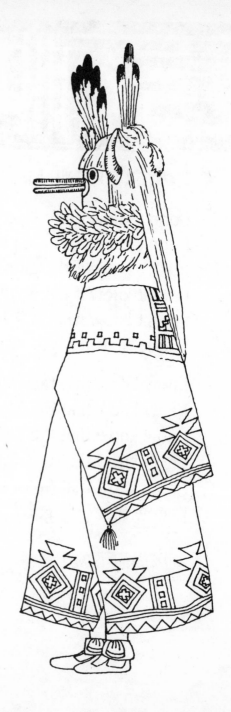

Prayers to the Natural World

The first man holds it in his hands
He holds the sun in his hands
In the center of the sky, he holds it in his hands
As he holds it in his hands, it starts upward.

The first Woman holds it in her hands
She holds the moon in her hands
In the center of the sky, she holds it in her hands
As she holds it in her hands, it starts upward.

∞ *Navajo prayer song*

I see the Earth.
I am looking at her and smile
Because she makes me happy.
The Earth, looking back at me
Is smiling too.
May I walk happily
And lightly
Upon Her.

∞ *Navajo prayer song*

Its feet, they are beautiful
Its legs, they are beautiful
Its body, it is beautiful
Its chest, it is beautiful
Its breast, it is beautiful
Its head feather, it is beautiful
The Earth is beautiful.

∞ *Navajo prayer song*

PRAYER TO THE SUN

Who among men and all creatures
Could live without the Sun Father?
For his light brings day, warms and
gladdens the Earth Mother with rain,
Which flows forth the water we drink.
And that causes the flesh of the
Earth Mother to yield seeds abundantly.

∞ *Zuni tribe*

Now the Mother Earth
And the Father Sky
Meeting, joining one another,
Helpmates ever, they.

All is beautiful,
All is beautiful,
All is beautiful,
Indeed.

∞ *Navajo prayer song*

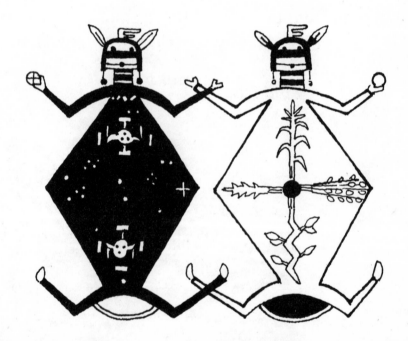

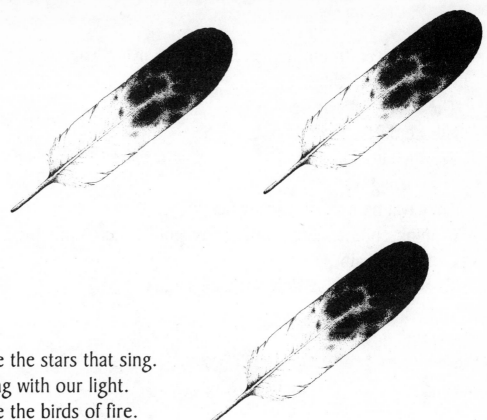

We are the stars that sing.
We sing with our light.
We are the birds of fire.
We fly across the heaven.
Our light is a star.

∞ *Passamaquoddy tribe*

When our earth mother is replete with living waters,
When spring comes,
The source of our flesh,
All the different kinds of corn,
We shall lay to rest in the ground with the earth mother's
        living waters.
They will be made into new beings,
Coming out standing into the daylight of their sun father,
Calling for rain.
To all sides they stretch out their hands…

∞ *Zuni prayer song*

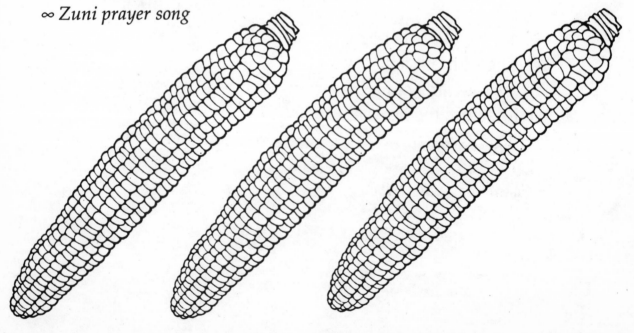

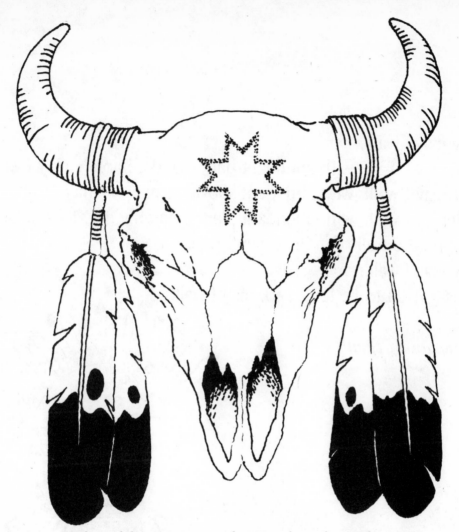

The old men say—the Earth only endures.
You spoke truly—you are right.

∞

Lakota song

35

Happily may I walk.
Happily may I walk, with abundant dark clouds, happily may I walk.
Happily may I walk, with abundant showers, happily may I walk.
Happily may I walk, with abundant plants, happily may I walk.
Happily, on the trail of pollen, may I walk.
Happily may I walk.
Being as it used to be long ago, may I walk.

∞ *Navajo prayer chant*

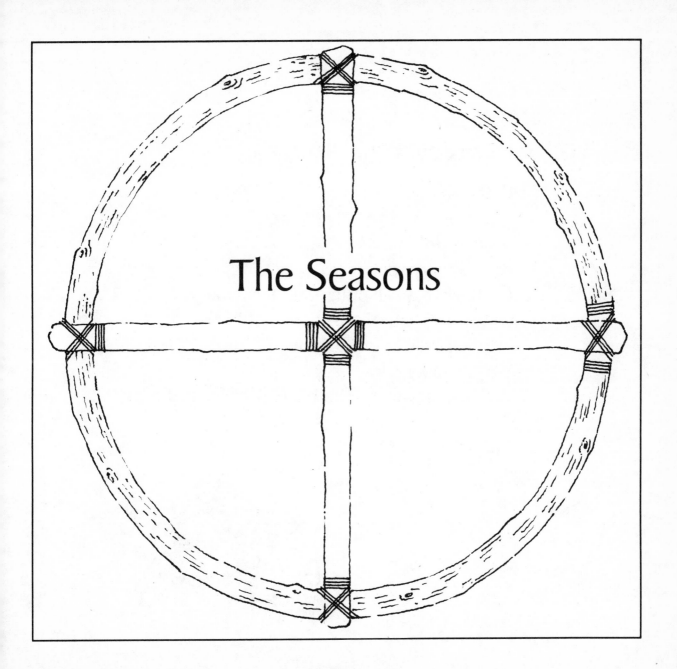

The Seasons

PRAYER OVER THE NEW SEEDS

In the Spring,
When your Earth Mother is wet,
In your Mother
You will bury your seeds.
Carefully they will bring forth their young.
Toward this your thoughts should focus.
Talking kindly to one another
We shall always live.
We shall pray that out roots may be fulfilled.

∞ *Zuni tribe*

SEED PRAYER

Watch well over your seed children!
Speak wisely to these our new children!
They will be your first speakers and the
peace-making shields of your people.

∞ *Zuni tribe*

Footprints I make! I go to the field with eager haste.
Footprints I make! Amid rustling leaves I stand.
Footprints I make! Amid yellow blossoms I stand.
Footprints I make! I stand exultant, proud.
Footprints I make! I hasten homeward with a burden of gladness.
Footprints I make! There is joy and gladness in my home.
Footprints I make! I stand amidst a day of contentment.

∞ *Osage Corn-Gatherers song*

It is a time of hunger,
But I don't feel like hunting.
I don't care for the advice of old people.
I only care for dreaming, wishing, nothing else.
I only care for gossip;
I am fond of young caribou; the age they start
        getting their antlers.
Nobody is like me.
I am too lazy, simply too lazy.
I just can't bring myself to go get some meat.

∞ *Aleut Winter Thoughts*

41

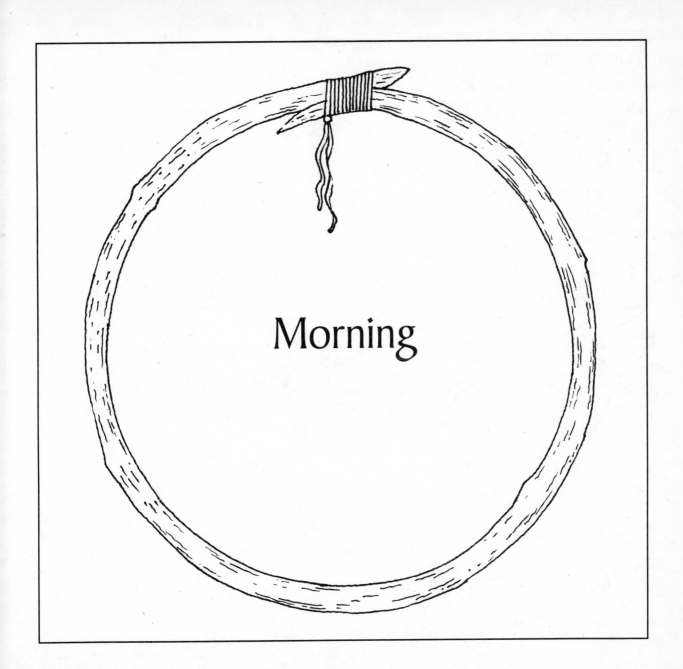

Morning

I am telling this.
Yonder the bear stands.
He faces the east just before
the sun appears.
Yonder the bear stands.
Now the sun is coming.

∞ *Pawnee tribe*

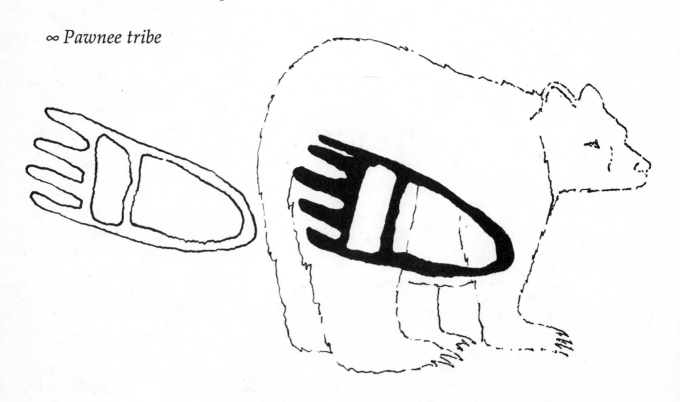

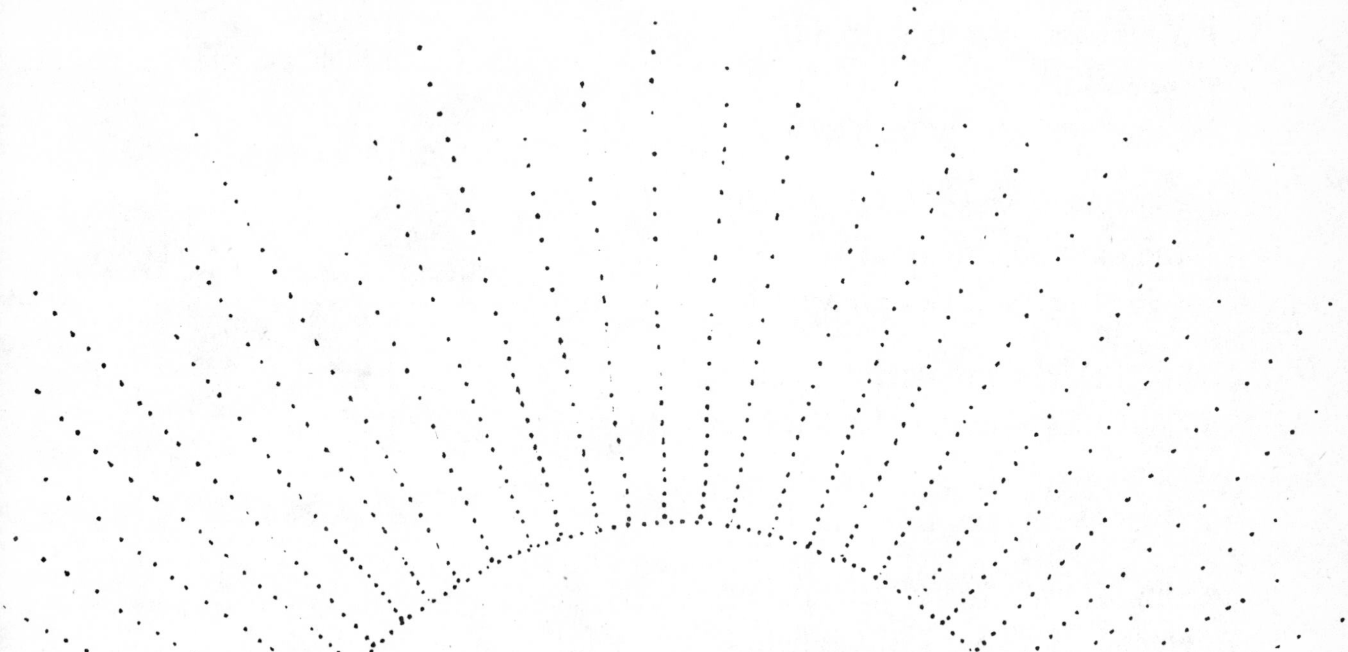

Day arises from its sleep.
Day wakes up with the dawning light.
Also you must arise. Also you must awake.
Together with the day which comes.

∞

Aleut song

MORNING PRAYER

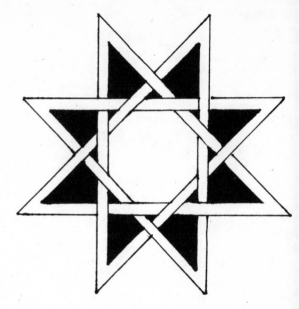

Morning Star, for you we watch!
Dimly comes your light from the distant sky.
We see you.
Morning Star, you bring life to us.

Morning Star, we see your brilliant shape.
Clothed in a shining body you come.
Morning Star, how you are vanishing.

Youthful Dawn, we watch for you.
Dimly comes your light from the distant sky.
We see you.
Youthful Dawn, you bring life to us.

Youthful Dawn, we see you coming.
Brighter grows your glowing light.
Nearer you come.
Youthful Dawn, now you are vanishing.

Day is here! The sun is here!
Arise and lift your eyes. Day is here!
Look up my children and see the day.
Day is here! Day is here!

∞ *Pawnee tribe*

My children, my children,
It is I who wear the morning star on my head,
It is I who wear the morning star on my head,
I show it to my children,
I show it to my children,
Says the father,
Says the father.

∞

Lakota Ghost Dance song

Eagle, come to us, with wings outspread in sunny skies!
Eagle, come to us, and bring us peace—gentle peace.
Eagle, come to us, and give new life to us who pray.

∞

Pawnee tribe

The Creator and Spirits

Here I do say,
>The one that is flying downward.

My fathers…

I saw it in its flight…

I tell of it,
>Above the heavens…

Now he comes among us,
>The one carrying lights as he flies…

Now it comes flying close to the ground…

I had a strange feeling,
>As this light flew along…

Now it was vanished in its flight.
>The star, the big one.

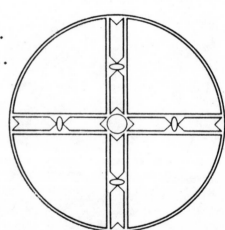

∞ *Pawnee tribe*

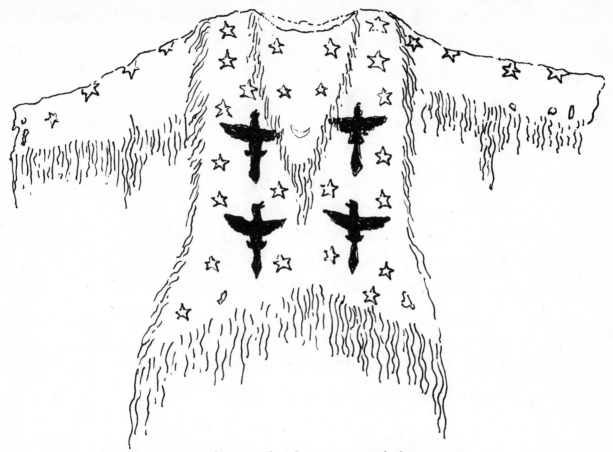

It is I who made these sacred things,
says the father, says the father.
It is I who make the sacred shirt,
says the father, says the father.

∞

Lakota Ghost Dance Song

51

Often in my travels I came to the land of Spirits.
As day approaches I travel and
    come to the land of the spirits.
Often in my travels I come to the land of Spirits.
As sun drops, I travel and come to the land of Spirits.
Often in my travels I come to the land of Spirits.
In my dreams I travel and come to the land of Spirits.
Often in my travels I come to the land of Spirits.
As a Spirit I travel and come to the land of Spirits.

∞ Osage Spirit song

In the center of the Sacred Mountain,
At the place called "Home in the Turning Rock,"
The Mountain Spirits, sacred, sacred,
Sing over me.
In the center of the Sacred Mountain,
Stands a brush shelter,
Home of the black Mountain Spirit.
With lightning flashing from my moccasins,
With lightning striking along my path,
My headdress lives.
Its jingles tinkling.
Its sound is heard!
My song embraces these dancers.

∞ *Apache Mountain Spirit song*

53

Above shall go
The spirits of people
Swaying rhythmically
Swaying with dandelion puffs in their hands.

∞ *Winter song*

I have passed you on the roads
My divine Father's life-giving breath
His breath of old age
His breath of the waters
His breath of seeds
His breath of riches
His breath of fecundity
His breath of power
His breath of good spirit

∞ *Navajo prayer song*

I circle around
I circle around
The boundaries of the earth
The boundaries of the earth
Wearing the long wing feathers as I fly
Wearing the long wing feathers as I fly

∞ *Arapaho Ghost Dance song*

THE SONG OF THE COYOTE WHO STOLE THE FIRE

I am frivolous Coyote; I wander around
I have seen the Black God's fire; I wander around
I stole his fire from him; I wander around
I have it! I have it!

I am changing Coyote; I wander around
I have seen the bumble-bee's fire; I wander around
I stole his fire from him; I wander around
I have it! I have it!

∞ *Navajo prayer song*

Let us see, is this real,
Let us see, is this real,
This life I am living?
Spirits, who dwell everywhere,
Let us see, is this real
This life I am living?

∞ *Pawnee song*

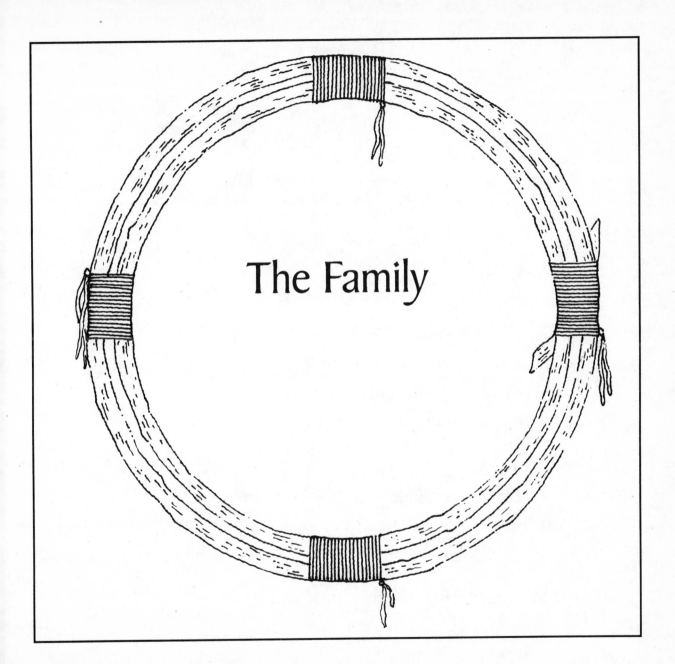

The Family

They were pure and clean and noble because
they had just come from the stars, say the holy men…
When they descended to earth, the Sacred One,
they found her divided into land and water…
They were quite modest before the mighty manifestations
of the Great Mysteries, and meek before Earth's anger and whims,
and referred to themselves as the little ones.

∞ *Osage tribal teaching*

Today we are blessed
With this beautiful baby.
May his feet be to the East
His right hand to the South
His head to the West
His left hand to the North.
May he walk and dwell on Mother Earth peacefully.
May he be blessed with assorted soft valued goods.
May he be blessed with precious variegated stones.
May he be blessed with fat sheep in variation.
May he be blessed with nice swift horses in variation.
May he be blessed with respectful relatives and friends.
I ask all these blessings with reverence and holiness.
My Mother, the Earth, the Sky, the Sun, the Moon,
     Together my Father.
I am the essence of life which is old age.
I am the source of happiness and beauty.
All is peaceful, all in beauty, all in happiness.
Now this is the day
Our child is blessed
Into the daylight.

∞ *Navajo prayer song*

61

TEWA LULLABY

There are many sleepy little birds,
Sleepy little birds, sleepy little birds.
So go to sleep, my little one.
Come down sleepy little birds, and
Sleep on her soft eyes.
That she may sleep the livelong day,
That she may sleep the livelong night.

∞ *Tewa tribe*

I make a baby board for you, my son.
May you grow to a great old age.
Of the rays of the earth, I make the back.
The blanket, I make of the black clouds.
The bow, I make of the rainbow.
The side-loops, I make of the sun beams.
The food board, I make of the sun dogs.
The covering, I make of the dawn.
The bed, I make of the black fog.

∞ *Navajo Blessing song*

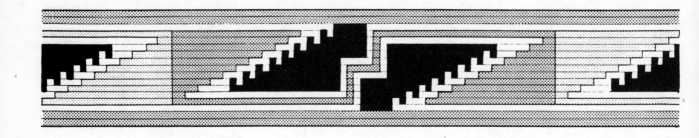

It is so still in the house
There is calm in the house;
The snowstorm wails out there,
And dogs are rolled up with noses under their tails.
My little boy is sleeping on the ledge,
On his back he lives, breathing through his mouth.
His little stomach is bulging round—
Is it strange if I start to cry with joy?

∞ *Aleut Mother's thoughts*

Here is a child
who has been given to us.
Let us bring him to manhood…
you who are dawn youths and dawn maidens.
You who are winter spirits.
You who are summer spirits.
Give him good fortune.
This we ask of you.

∞

Tewa prayer

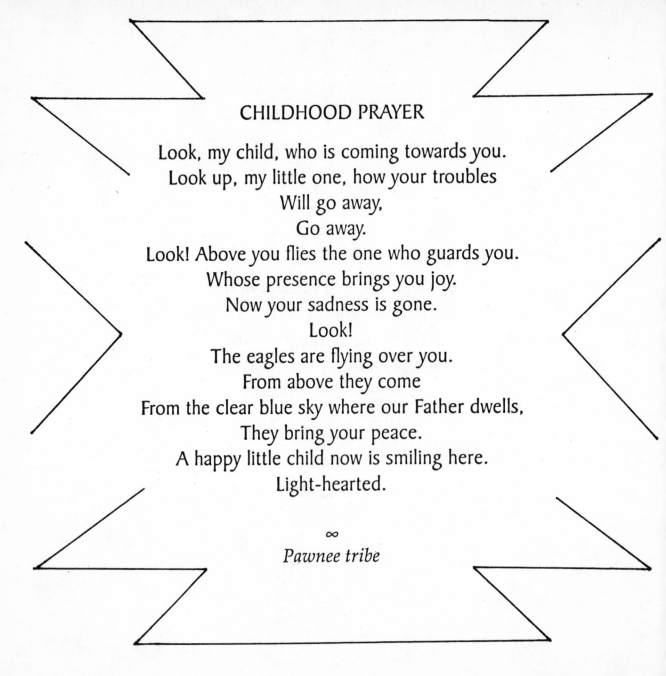

CHILDHOOD PRAYER

Look, my child, who is coming towards you.
Look up, my little one, how your troubles
Will go away,
Go away.
Look! Above you flies the one who guards you.
Whose presence brings you joy.
Now your sadness is gone.
Look!
The eagles are flying over you.
From above they come
From the clear blue sky where our Father dwells,
They bring your peace.
A happy little child now is smiling here.
Light-hearted.

∞

Pawnee tribe

ADOPTION PRAYER AND BLESSING

Friend, this day I take you in my arms and hug you strongly.
And if it is meant to be,
Our Father the sun will, in his path over the world,
rise and reach his zenith,
Hold himself firmly and smile upon you and me
that our roads of life may be finished.
Here I touch you with my hand
and with the hands and hearts of the gods.
I pray to the wind of life,
That our roads of life may be finished together.
Friend, may the light of the gods meet you!

∞

Zuni tribe

My breath, I have it here
My bones, I have them here
My flesh, I have them here
With it I seek you
With it I find you
But speak to me
Say something nice to me.

∞ *Aleut love song*

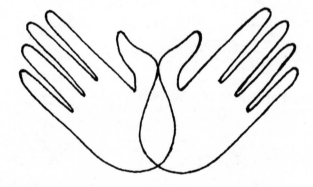

Blessings

May there be happiness
May there be success
May there be good health
May there be well being

∞

Navaho chant

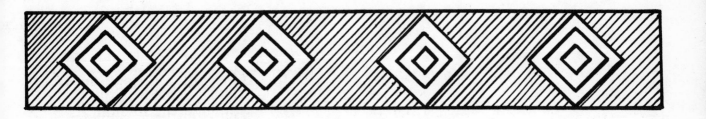

BLESSING

May the Great Spirit send his choicest gifts to you,
May the Sun Father and the Moon Mother shed
their softest beams on you,
May the Four Winds of the World blow gently upon you and
Upon those with whom you share your heart and home.

∞

Coahuila tribe

SONG OF THE SKY LOOM

Mother Earth, Father Sky,
We are your children.
We bring you the offerings that you love.
We form a blanket of brightness.
May the warp be the white light of morning.
May the weft be the red light of evening.
May the fringes be of the falling rain.
May the border be the arching rainbow.
Weave for us a blanket of brightness,
So that we can walk in the way that the birds sing,
So that we can walk in the green grass.
Mother Earth, Father Sky.

∞ *Tewa tribe*

Our sun father
Went in to sit down at his sacred place.
And our night fathers,
Having come out standing to their sacred place,
Passing a blessed night
We came today.
Now this day.

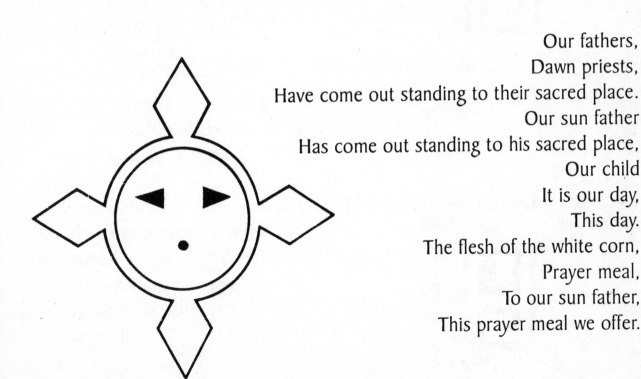

Our fathers,
Dawn priests,
Have come out standing to their sacred place.
Our sun father
Has come out standing to his sacred place,
Our child
It is our day,
This day.
The flesh of the white corn,
Prayer meal,
To our sun father,
This prayer meal we offer.

May your road be fulfilled
Reaching to the road of your sun father.
When your road is fulfilled
In your thought (May we live).
May we be the ones whom your thoughts will embrace,

For this, on this day
To our sun father.
His breath of all good things whatsoever,
Asking for his breath,
And into my warm body
Drawing his breath,
I add to your breath now.
Let no one despise the breath of his fathers.
But into your bodies,
Draw their breath,
That yonder to where the road of our sun father comes out,
Your roads may reach.
That clasping hands,
Holding one another fast,
You may finish your roads,
To this end, I add to your breath now.

Verily, so long as we enjoy the light of day,
May we greet each other with love;
Verily, so long as we enjoy the light of day,
May we pray for one another...
Through the winter,
Through the summer,
Throughout the cycle of the months,
I have prayed for light for you.
Now this day,
I have fulfilled their thoughts,
Perpetuating the rite of our father,
Sayataca bow priest,
And giving him human form.

∞ *Zuni prayer song*

Looking Westward:
"Over there are the mountains.
May you gaze upon them as long as
you live.
From there you will get your Sweet-
Pine as incense."

Looking Northward:
"Over there is The-Star-that-never-
moves
From the North will come your
strength.
May you see the Star for many
years."

Looking Eastward:
"Over there is Old Age.
From that Direction comes the light
of Sun."

Looking Southward:
"May warm winds from the South
bring you plenty of food."

∞

Pikuni Good-Luck song

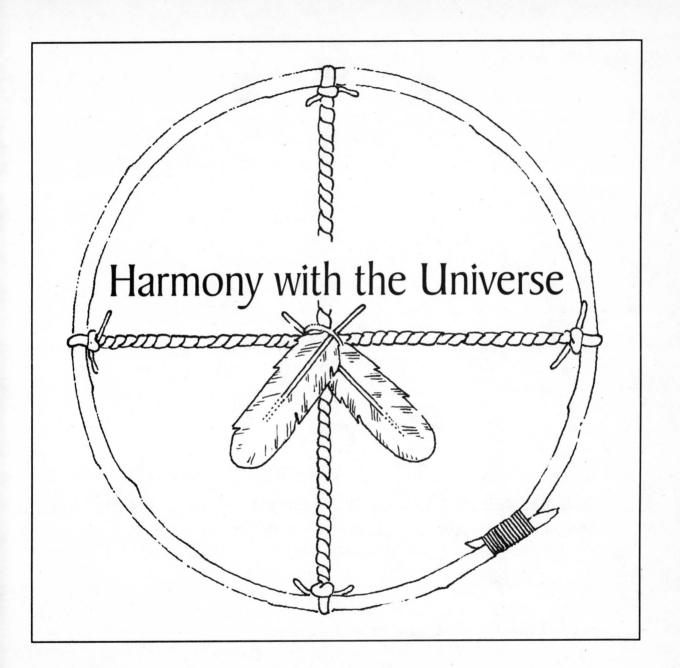

Harmony with the Universe

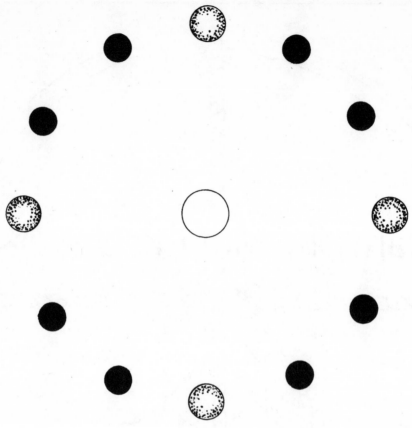

Peace…comes within the souls of men when they realize their
relationship, their oneness, with the universe and all its powers,
and when they realize that at the center of the Universe
dwells Wakan-tanka, and that this center is everywhere,
it is within each of us.

∞ *Black Elk, Oglala Lakota tribe*

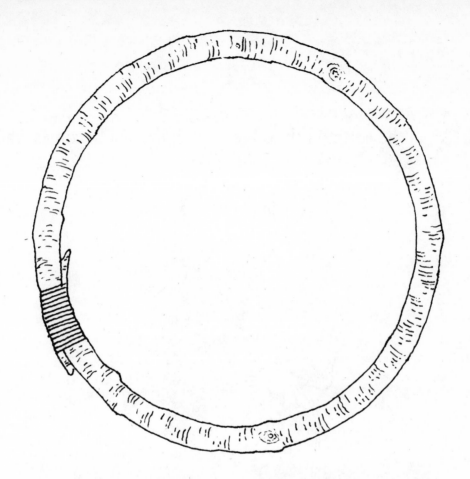

My words are tied in one with the great mountains,
with the great rocks, with the great trees.
In one with my body and my heart.

∞

Yokuts prayer

The wise man who meditates on the goodness of all that exists in the sky, in the earth, in the lakes, and in the sea becomes whole.

∞

Mayan saying

The mountains, I become part of it...
The herbs, the fir tree, I become part of it.
The morning mists, the clouds, the gathering waters,
I become part of it.
The wilderness, the dew drops, the pollen...
I become part of it.

∞ *Navajo prayer song*

81

SONG OF CREATING PEOPLE

The Earth, its life am I, hozhoni, hozhoni
The Earth, its feet are my feet, hozhoni, hozhoni
The Earth, its legs are my legs, hozhoni, hozhoni
The Earth, its body is my body, hozhoni, hozhoni
The Earth, its thoughts are my thoughts, hozhoni, hozhoni
The Earth, its speech is my speech, hozhoni, hozhoni
The Earth, it down-feathers are my down-feathers,
hozhoni, hozhoni.

∞ *Navajo prayer song*

Listen to her...
to our Earth, our Mother,
to what she is saying.
People, listen all.

∞

Mohawk prayer

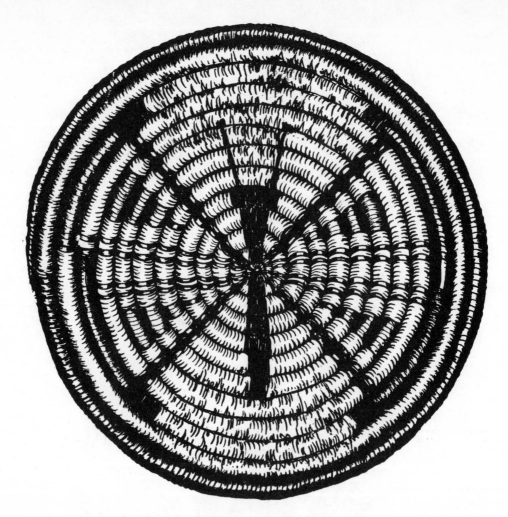

The land…it is a mother; a living thing to us that produces food and other living things. You cannot deny anyone from sharing it… I pray for all living things to go on.

∞ *Mina Lansa, Hopi tribe*

This covers it all
The earth and the Most High Power
Whose ways are Beautiful.

All is beautiful before me,
All is beautiful behind me,
All is beautiful above me,
All is beautiful around me.

This covers it all,
The skies and the Most High Power
Whose ways are beautiful.
All is beautiful.

∞ *Navajo prayer song*

85

Look, I see the Sun…
He is my father
He is my beginning
Look, I see the Moon…
She is my Grandmother
      my guardian keeper
Look, I see the stars…
They are my friends,
      my relatives
Look, I see the universe…
      I see myself.

∞ High Eagle, Osage/Cherokee tribes

House made of dawn.
House made of evening light.
House made of the dark cloud.
House made of male rain.
House made of dark mist.
House made of female rain.
House made of pollen.
House made of grasshoppers.

Dark cloud is at the door.
The trail out of it is dark cloud.
The zig zag lightning stands high upon it.
An offering I made.

∞ *Navajo prayer song*

That flowing water!
That flowing water!
    My mind wanders across it.
That broad water!
That broad water!
    My mind wanders across it.
That old age water!
That flowing water!
    My mind wanders across it.

∞ *Navajo song*

It was the wind that gave them life.
It was the wind that comes out of our mouths
    that gives us life.
When this ceases to blow we die.
In the skin at the tips of our fingers we see the
    trail of the wind.
It shows us the wind blew when our ancestors
    were created.

∞ *Navajo chant*

Restore my feet for me.
Restore my legs for me.
Restore my body for me.
Restore my mind for me.
Restore my voice for me.
This very day take out your spell for me.

Happily I recover.
Happily my interior becomes cool.
Happily I go forth.
My interior feeling cool, may I walk
No longer sore, may I walk
As it used to be long ago, may I walk.

∞ *Navajo prayer song*

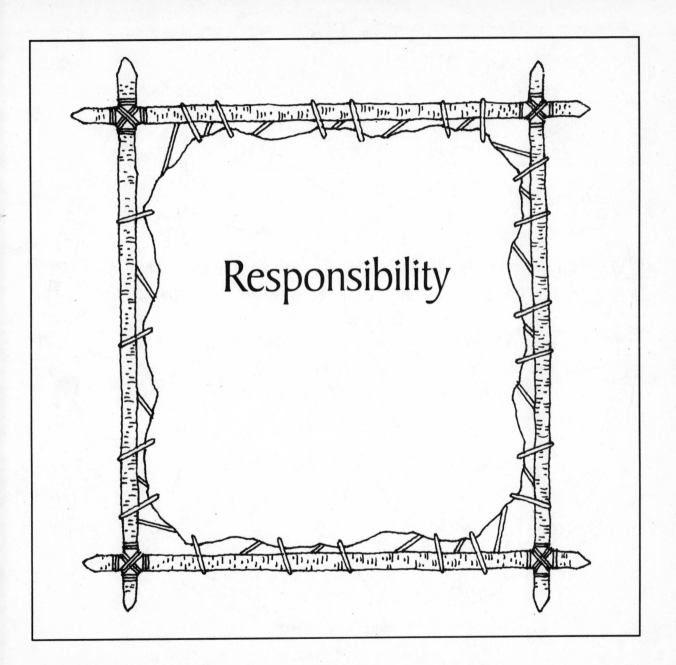

Responsibility

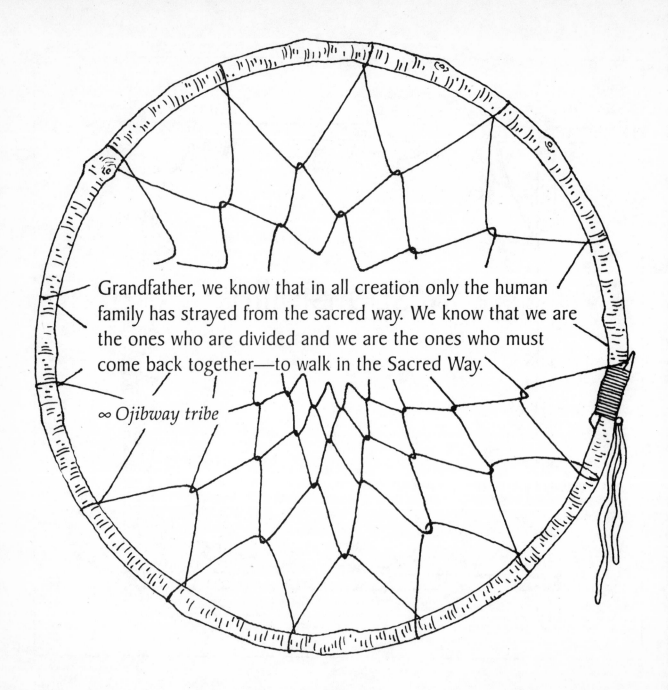

Grandfather, we know that in all creation only the human family has strayed from the sacred way. We know that we are the ones who are divided and we are the ones who must come back together—to walk in the Sacred Way.

∞ *Ojibway tribe*

We are all aware that here, as well as other places, certain mystical changes are occurring in society, causing us to question our very basis of existence. Some of us know the sacred purposes and designs given to us by our creator and realize that the spirit dwells within all of us. But unfortunately, some other people, giving way to great ambitions, are trying to control others. Instead of correcting certain imbalances for today's world, they are busy trading blame which further drains our planet of spiritual energy. These people are weaving self-destructive circles, causing great harm to all land and life.

It is a fact that today's generation no longer relies on what was said by our forefathers. They have forgotten how to avoid temptation— a key by which man has survived thus far. And while it is true that we cannot escape new changes, we can at least use these changes wisely, so that we won't destroy those important elements which maintain our way of life. At this point in time, we must awaken ourselves to our true destiny.

∞ *Jack Pongyayesva, Hopi elder*

Our religious teachings are based upon the proper care of our land and the people who live upon it. We must not lose the way of life of our religion if we are to remain Hopis. We believe in that: we live it, day by day. We do not want to give it up for the way of another. For the benefit of our people throughout the land, and for the people to come after us in our land, and for those who care to learn, we Hopis want to be known among other people throughout all other lands as the Hopi, the people of Peace. Let all people hear our voice.

∞ *Andrew Hermequaftewa, Hopi tribe*

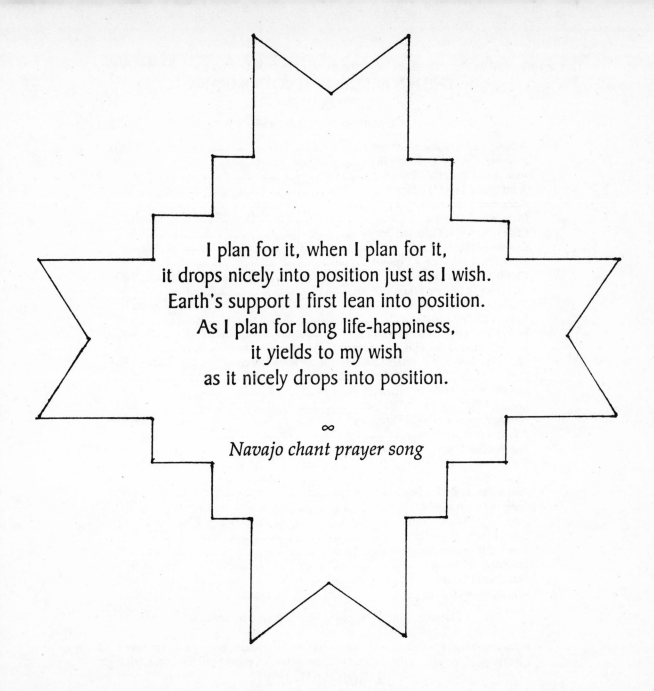

I plan for it, when I plan for it,
it drops nicely into position just as I wish.
Earth's support I first lean into position.
As I plan for long life-happiness,
it yields to my wish
as it nicely drops into position.

∞

Navajo chant prayer song

These fine Native American books are available from your local bookstore or from:
THE BOOK PUBLISHING COMPANY
PO BOX 99
Summertown TN 38483

A Basic Call to Consciousness	$7.95
American Indian Coloring Book	3.00
Arts & Crafts of the Cherokee	9.95
Aunt Mary Tell Me a Story	3.95
Blackfoot Craftworker's Book	11.95
Chants and Prayers	9.95
Cherokee A B C Coloring Book	3.00
Cherokee Plants	3.95
The Cherokees Past & Present	3.95
Children of the Circle	9.95
Daughters of Abya Yala	8.95
Dream Feather	11.95
Eyes of Chief Seattle	16.95
Finger Weaving: Indian Braiding	4.95
A Good Medicine Collection: Life in Harmony with Nature	10.95
How Can One Sell the Air? Chief Seattle's Vision (Revised)	6.95
How to Make Cherokee Clothing	23.95
Indian Tribes of the Northern Rockies	9.95
Legends Told by the Old People	5.95
Native American Crafts Directory	8.95
A Natural Education	8.95
The People: Native American Thoughts and Feelings	5.95
The Powwow Calendar	8.95
Sacred Song of the Hermit Thrush	5.95
Seven Clans of the Cherokee Society	3.95
Song of Seven Herbs	11.95
Song of the Wild Violets	5.95
Spirit of the White Bison	5.95
Story of the Cherokee People	3.95
Teachings of Nature	8.95
Traditional Dress	6.95
Where Legends Live	5.95

Please include $2.50 per book additional for shipping.

If you are interested in other fine books on Native Americans, ecology, alternative health, gardening, vegetarian cooking and childrens' books, please call for a free catalog:
1-800-695-2241